Turnpike Prairie

Kerry Moyer

Kellogg Press   Topeka, KS

Published by Kellogg Press
Topeka, KS
www.kelloggpress.com

Curtis Becker, Editor/Design
curtis@curtisbeckerbooks.com

Printed in the United States of America

Rockwell Font
Adobe Georgia Font

Curtis Becker and Kevin Rabas, Photography
Mick Ball, Location Scouting

ISBN: 978-0-578-96487-4

"Fireflies" and "Mass Street" originally apeared in *Astra Magazine*, December 2020.

Turnpike Prairie

One day I will find the right words,
and they will be simple.

-Jack Kerouac

Table of Contents

Drving
Turnpike Prairie   2
Grasses   3
Cold Drink, Crackers, and Twenty Dollars in Gas   4
Carburetor   5
Twelve Miles West of Santa Rosa New Mexico   6
High Desert   7

Pandemic
Mask   10
Spring   11
[In & Out]   12
Aisle Dance   13
[April 2020: A Bike Ride]   14
Lighthouse   15
A Tuesday   16
                                                        17

Family
Bend
[in bed]   20
Kettle Drum   21
Hammers   22
[claws]   23
Prime   24
Two Deer   25
A Walk   26

Fire
[fire pit out back]   28
[we gather]   29
To Sit Before a Fire   30
[my wife stirs]   31
[spent log]   32

Body

Bionic   70
Bloody Knuckles   71
Give Me Shoes   72
[shower at 11:42 pm on a Tuesday]   73
Sbower Chair   74
[man in the...]   75
Middle Age   76

Mind

[this box]   78
Home   79
Concrete Shoes   80
Wasteland   81
Surface Tension   82
Hamster Wheel   83
Waves   84
Rivulets   85
Tenpenny Nail   86
Broken Notes   87
[insomnia]   88
[ballerina]   89

Soul

Sacred   92
[God, sometimes]   93
Lost   94
Dying   95
Live and Let Live   96
If I Met the Devil   97
[in church]   98
Square Window   99
Rings   100

Moyer Musings

Like Morning   102
Coffee   103
Sharp Edges   104
Chewing Sounds   105
Letter Jackets   106
Fireflies   107
Flim-Flam   108
Wooden Box   109
Trench Warfare   110

A Kansas Life

[sitting in my truck at a railroad crossing]   112
Leaves   113
Sidewlk Quiet   114
Trees in the Fall   115
[Do you shop here often?]   116
God & Lattes]   117
Fortune Cookie   118
Red Barn   119
Garden Song   120
One Day   121
Prairie Heart   122

Driving

Turnpike Prairie

Toll road runs North and South,
a vein, snaking through the Flint Hills.
Limestone shown through tallgrass
that changes with each passing season.
Weathered billboards tell folks to stop here,
buy that, while a midwestern sky, and all
of it's moods stretch out over highway signs,
mile-markers and power lines.

Hopeful travelers count the hours
and children ask when they will arrive.
Wandering eyes look past fence lines,
spy rolling cattle pastures, watershed ponds.
Rows of many-colored cars, Jeeps,
pick-ups, semi-trucks carry the blood
of a country, through this
Kansas Turnpike prairie.

Grasses

Traveling north in late December,
my wife drives our maroon mini- van
down the interstate, white dashes
separate us from those moving
faster on our left, faster.
We move past tan grasses resting
dormant on each side of this road.
They are still, soft to my eyes, reaching
out in front of us, Keith Jarrett plays
in my ear, my heart,
My boys sit behind us lost
in their devices, maybe thoughts
like children, like books barely
started and my words scrolled
in their pages. Speed limit sign
says 60 mph, and I think,
How many miles? faster--
Those days moving past
like still frames and the tan,
dormant grasses watch, wait
for spring, for rain, for change.
My wife drives, facing forward
and I wonder if she sees
the grasses like I do.

Cold Drink, Crackers, and Twenty Dollars in Gas

Whistle breaks the quiet,
rolling down steel rails,
red and white striped gate,
flashing red lights,
coming white glow
steady roar of turning wheels.

I sit in my truck,
feeling the rumble
moving through everything,
rattling the change in my cab,
cold drink in my hand.

Watching colored train cars,
sun bleached, rusty and scarred,
reds, greens, browns, blues,
inner city modern art,
spray can masterpieces,
steady stream of rectangles
for just under two whole songs.

As the last car passes,
giving rise to the gate
and the end of flashing red lights,
an empty pull on my straw,
tells me it's time to go to Casey's
for another cold drink, crackers
and twenty dollars in gas.

Carburetor

The cast iron carburetor casing
is shedding red paint after days
of sitting in a bucket of gas. I
take a razor, scrape away black
crumbling gaskets, check clogged
ports with a needle, spray solvent
from a can to eat away rust, grease.
This old carb will get new parts, new
red paint, and my antique tractor
will run like it did seventy-four
years ago. I stop to think upon
my body, this worn out machine,
with rickety parts that will never
see a revival, a chance to be
like new. Seeing the time, I wipe
oil from aching hands, toss
the soiled towel on my bench,
lay down my battered wrench
and head inside my house
to rest.

Twelve Miles West of Santa Rosa New Mexico

Heading west,
twelve miles outside
of Santa Rosa,
New Mexico. We sat
on Route 66, broke
down. Luke's red
280-Z with a burned
up clutch, heading
to Arizona, and we
were high, hungry, cold,
listening to Cohen,
talking Jesus, how we
were broken, how we
were going to get
our gold. We chain
smoked Camels, drank
truck stop coffee,watched
that long,stretch of road
for anyone to drive
by, and I'm thinking,
I just need food,
sleep. Jail would
be alright this night.
We watched a sun
rise, bringing orange
and red over a high
desert sky. One car
coming, and it's the law.
White car flips red
lights and pulls
a u-turn, while Luke
ate the weed and I hid
my knife.

High Desert

Canopy of stars hung
over black mountains
in the high desert of New
Mexico, like a sparkling, dark
curtain and it was cold,
quiet, while I drove miles
on a straight stretch of road,
alone, a carton of Camels,
my thoughts and Leonard
Cohen singing to pass
time, these quiet
desert miles.

Pandemic

Kerry Moyer

Mask

My mask is cloth,
fashioned from
a handkerchief.
My wife's mask
has pink flowers,
Our boys have
ninja turtle masks
and ask us when
we can throw them
in the trash. When
we can go to stores,
feel safe, see smiles,
see faces again.

Spring

Green grass grows,
mower's in the garage
breeze blows warm
while the virus keeps
people scared, sheltered
inside.

Spring rolls in
and people wait
for this season to pass,
for this time to pass,
like a hard,
cruel winter.

[In & Out]

Everyone is edgy,
big-eyed. They rush
in, and rush out, pull on
long rubber gloves,
strap on cloth masks,
wipe cart handles
with disinfectant wipes.
I see this checker
who's probably making
ten bucks an hour.
Her eyes tired, above
her plain white mask,
no smile under there.
She goes to work,
like shaking a fist
and rolling a set of dice.

Aisle Dance

We do that weird aisle
dance, six feet between,
reaching at what little
is there. No toilet paper
or rice, no smiles, worried
eyes. Coronavirus in March.
People lining up, hoping
no one coughs, no one
gets too close.

Kerry Moyer

[April 2020: A Bike Ride]

Riding my bike, I'm pushing
pedals past quiet houses, alone, not
a soul outside. I catch an eerie feeling
rolling down quiet Covid streets, I think
people are in their homes, walling
the world out, scared of the air,
in April, 2020.

Lighthouse

Foaming seas crash
against rock, against
my days, my thoughts
and fog covers my eyes
while I look for hope
in these dark days,
no lighthouse to see
me through this
troubled May.

Kerry Moyer

A Tuesday

I hear computer keys click
from my son's room
and I know he spends
little time with friends
face to face, but online
they talk through mics,
look at screens because
Covid came and locked
us in houses, in rooms,
in wait, and I'm not sure
what the day is, so I ask
my son, who looks up,
says, "Tuesday, dad,
I think it's Tuesday"
and looking away
goes back to his
glowing device.

Bend

Waking, I scroll
the news feed,
see growing
numbers of sick,
growing death
numbers, drink
my coffee while
the earth bends,
our lives bend
under Covid-19
and we wait, hope
that curve goes
flat, those numbers
fall, before we
can't bend,
and it all
breaks.

Family

Kerry Moyer

[in bed]

Side by side and it's
quiet, but for the soft
tap of fingers on small
glowing screens, the sound
of my white fan
droning is comfort.
Twenty years, we've gone
to our marriage bed.
Some nights my wife
and I, separated
by acres of blankets
and other nights,
by inches of sheets,
but we sleep.
We always
go to sleep.

Kettle Drum

My life,
a winding river,
flowing through days,
the rhythm of each place,
my people in their time
come and go, my children
they will grow beyond me
and my kettle drum heart
will beat with the force
of love, of time and an end
that will slowly fade, but for
the sake of memory.

Hammers

She has hard
words to throw like
hammers, end over
end, tumbling, and I
dodge the claws,
the flat face, tumbling,
and I think, What the hell
do I say? If I just had
a script, some clever
words to spit, or just
didn't give a shit,
then I'd just let
those claws, those
flat faces fall
to the floor.

[claws]

My cat can be so still, watching birds
through glass, or sleeping for hours,
but for the occasional stretch
in this window that holds his eyes,
and mine. I think with a hungry grin,
I'm like a cat, wanting to stretch my claws.

Kerry Moyer

Prime

Miles comes in
my room, shows me
his Optimus Prime
and like a wizard
genius engineer,
transforms the toy
from truck to warrior
then says "Dad, Optimus
Prime is a nice guy
and brave like you."
I tell him "son, Prime
is my hero too"
and he grins
says "well of course"
with a Miles smile
of approval.

Two Deer

Two deer,
one smaller
than the other, walk
across a distant field,
trees stand, like a wall,
behind them. Sarah's
in her kitchen unpacking
her pots, pans, I hear
the clang of dishes. Our
boys are busying themselves
in their new bedrooms. I drink
strong coffee from my thrown
blue mug, and look out across
my new yard, green grass, trees,
cup in hand and I smile from my
new front porch, and a feeling
of calm comes over me, while
those deer move freely,
disappearing
from my
view.

A Walk

A red car drives by slow.
There Is Cuban jazz coming
from its window and in spite
of my low mood, I smiled.
I had messaged my son that I'm
walking to look for him
because I wanted to see him,
because I love him and time
is on my mind. He messaged back
that he wanted to walk alone.
I walked for a while and he
typed to me that he is walking
the same road I am and I
kind of thought to myself,
there is more truth in that
than he knows right now.
Around a corner,
by a darkened school,
his lanky frame stood, in a black
hoodie and we met to finish
this evening walk that we
both started alone.

Fire

Kerry Moyer

[fire pit out back]

I hauled in Arkansas sandstone, red
and brown, and Sarah and the boys
and I stacked rocks, hollowed
a pit for the fire, poured gas
from a can, and lit the wood.
Night, and the fire
lights on our faces like ancient paint
across cave walls,
and after six or seven days straight
with a shovel, I've settled, like wheat
dust on a fresh cut field.

with Kevin Rabas

[we gather]

I dug up rock from hard earth,
dropped sweat like hot rain
from a salty, soiled forwhead
onto Arkansas stones stacked
in a circle for logs to burn
on cool Autumn nights.
We gather here
for quiet,
for light,
for heat.

To Sit Before a Fire

To sit before a fire,
my thoughts, a pyre
aflame, each word
like matchsticks
struck, burning,
writing a primitive
song on my heart,
like all men who sit
before a fire with
a heart aflame.

[my wife stirs]

My wife stirs
the fire with a stick,
embers are white hot,
a flame twists in her eyes,
the fire bends, while she
moves wood, coals
that burn, flames
like sirens, drawing
me to heat.

Kerry Moyer

[spent log]

Tonight, I'm a spent
log from a fire, black
carbon ash brought
to its present state
by time and heat,
by the fiery spark,
the air I breathe.

Growing Up

Kerry Moyer

[nowhere to go]

That brown leather belt
was whirling, curving, came
down on my back, my chest
like a thick, hot whip, leaving
burning, stinging welts.

Pulling arms and legs in tight,
I couldn't get small enough
and there was nowhere to go.

Wonton Soup

Phoenix served wonton soup,
looked me in the eye,
asked if he'd been drinking,
if he'd blown the rent.

I looked away, said yes,
lifted the spoon to my lips.

Later, father threw me against
the neighbor's house, cocked
his fist. I cocked my eyes, cocked
my mouth, said, "Do it, and you
will never see me again!"
He broke. He cried.

I walked to Casey's
for a coke, dried my tears,
wiped rage from my eyes.

The Cat that Ate the Canary

Dad moved to Wichita
To sell cars and got
a place with Jimmy.
This one time Jimmy
got high on cocaine,
broke his leg doing
karate in the shower.

Jimmy sold used cars,
drank cheap whiskey,
owned an Atari, played
Pac-man, talked about
the hustle, was always
grinning like the cat
that ate the canary.

[watercolor]

Watercolor houses
lined watercolor streets,
under watercolor skies,
all the edges bleed
together, turning the reds
and blues to purple, blues
and yellows to green, faces
to sagging masks looking
out sagging windows. My
watercolor memories wander
to Warren Road, and I'm a boy
running, wearing watercolor shoes.

Boot

The house had mud, silt
an inch deep on wooden
floors.
The wild yard held long
grasses, weeds.
Father walked slow,
brooding.
Our rental house flooded
by big rain that fell
for days.
In the garage, I moved
wet boxes full
of trash and there
I found new, pink
babies bunched, moving.
Father comes, looks
down, says "mice", wipes
his head with a savage
hand, crushes them under
a soiled, brown boot.
I cried while he walked
away,
without another word.

Two Rooms

He moved
between two rooms.
Sunlight came in through
two windows, one
in each room.
He didn't look out
but every now and then,
when a noise drew
his ears, when light
drew his eyes.
He carried this sadness
that kept him moving
from one room
to the other,
wearing a path
between,
on a scratched
wooden floor,
no desire to wander
out of doors.
His wife, children
downstairs, hearing
the pacing, waiting,
hoping to hear him
walk down the stairs.

Leaving Arizona

I was leaving Arizona
and went to tell him.
Father wept on his porch,
sitting in a chair, shaking.
I can still see his eyes,
his tears and right now
I miss what little we had.

Time

I held his hand while
the sound of air, machine
clicks timed with crackles
that came from his hard
breaths and he asked me
for time and I had none
to give, no magic
and he knew but
asked anyway.

Plastic Boats

The curb ran long and straight,
clear down the street to a curve,
rain water flowed like a river
carrying my plastic yellow boat
while I gave chase to save the craft
from the gutter that claimed my red
boat the year before, and untold
others, from untold neighborhood
kids. If legends told stories of anxious
youth on rainy days, waiting with plastic
boats ready to race down concrete
curbed rivers, then I'd have a part,
all my own.

Shred

My deck, scarred,
paint thrashed,
streaks on concrete,
skinned knees, elbows,
worn like badges.
Feral teens, rolling
down streets, skating
drainage ditches.
We'd grind, rail slide
in parking lots
and cops would run
us off while we used
words like shred,
like the rebel
heart of youth.

Kerry Moyer

[slow walk to the high school fight]

Slow walk
to the train
tracks by this
clearing of trees,
where I will square
up with Jones, pinch
closed my fists.
Blood pumps. I can
feel my pulse in my
fingers, my breathing
loud, but I'm light
on my feet.
Jones walks
ahead, but glances
back, and I see it,
his fear, cold, like frost
on his shoulders.
He stutter steps, stops,
says, "Do we have to do
this?" I tell him we do, "Should
have thought about that
before." We keep
walking, slow walking
to the clearing
besides where the tracks
come together, a weaving,
a twining, like with snakes.

with Kevin Rabas

[that wax]

Grandma kept a brown crock
pot close.
We would dip our
pencils in.
Grandpa told us
"That wax
is for grandma's hands,"
her twisted
fingers, cramped.
She would rub one
hand upon another
and moan, and we
would leave
her alone.

with Kevin Rabas

Farm in December

The farm looks different
in December.

White over red
earth, no green, creek
icy-still, gnarled branches
on gnarled trees.

Chickens cooped in wood,
wire, and straw. Pigs
penned. Cattle gathered
at the salt licks, tongues
out, the ground frozen over.

With the long hot days of harvest
two seasons away, machines rest
blanketed, whitened. Grandpa smokes
on the porch in his tattered gray
coat, pipe at his lip, while grandma
sits with her yarn at the scuffed
kitchen table, counting.

North Eighty

Rows of golden wheat sprung slow
from red earth on the North Eighty.
I sit wide eyed, watch for rabbits
that dash away from combine jaws.

Waving heads wait for the Red Massey
harvester to grab those golden grains,
fresh-cut kernels pass through a long-necked
auger that spits them into a filling bin.

The machine roars while grandpa holds
the wheel, drawing on his pipe, sending
tobacco smoke to dance with dust
under the faded yellow buggy top.

A blue sky dips with the setting sun.
Running lights come on for the last few
passes that will clear this field
and close the day.

I think back to this when my heart
yearns for fields, for wheat dust falling
like memories, like a summer harvest
living in the blue skies of my youth.

Red Tomatoes

Red tomatoes
from the garden, picked,
placed into a wicker basket
on the counter, and grandpa asks,
Would you like to take some home?
Grandpa's blue eyes over the top
of glasses, his busy hands already
finding the plastic bag,
and I would say "yes," like always,
for love, for him to give, for me
to receive, from his garden,
and then coffee,
the news of the day,
before grandpa would go
to his recliner and nap.

[Monday phone call]

My brother who
beat drugs again,
found some hope,
just called to say
he has a mass
on his lung, tells
me if he's got cancer
and dies, at least
he won't die
a junkie. In his voice,
a calm, like a cool
breeze, like a quiet
summer morning
and my tears, like
rain on this warm
Monday evening.

Empty Lot

The empty lot held my eyes,
stairs, grandpa's leather chair,
with that ash tray, fishing
magazines, a candy jar full
of sweet orange slices
that grandma gave in love
and they are gone for years
and this sacred spot holds
a wooden ghost with rooms
I know, and no steel machines
can tear those walls, those
square rooms, high above,
at the top of stairs,
on the edge of this
blue sky.

In Songs

I was listening to a song
when the words led to
thoughts and then to
faces. People I loved
and they are gone
and that feeling welled
up in my chest and
my father's face when
he was in his hospital
bed and grandpa working
in his garden and
grandma slipping me
a five-dollar bill
at Christmas
and I felt the losses
like they were new
again and I missed
their faces and their
voices and them
being in the world,
and now they are all
in songs.

Friends

Sweet

This Cola is ***sweet***,
dark,
established 1891.
Sitting in "Sign of Life"
Cafe
My company is ***sweet***.
Kevin, Curtis, we sit,
write cafe words, the guy
behind me looks agitated,
exasperated, and I'm
thinking, What's that
story?
And I'm ***sweet***, not bitter,
first day in three that felt
Good...
and I wish agitated, exasperated
guy would finish his coffee
and leave.

Sauce

Seventeen napkins dirty,
barbecue **sauce**, with greed,
blood sugar **sauce**, spicy, saucy,
sauce and bacon with gouda
cheese, melted, on a burger,
I'm a burger connoisseur,
seventeen napkins, dirty
with **sauce**, **sauce** on my
chin, in my beard
at a burger joint in LFK.

Kerry Moyer

Mass Street

Mass Street--
beatnik heaven, homeless
guy begs, bearded guy plays
his guitar for wadded up singles,
Quick, half- hearted smiles, pity,
shitty parking, but the place
is alive, Lawrence is alive, moving
businesses pulse with people
Lawrence, jittery with people,
like the buzz of bees,
around cars, light posts,
words on signs, windows,
doors, and a writer I know
passes by, says "hi," melts
back into the crowded sidewalk,

Friday Night at Mul's

Off work,
bar of fine folks
I know, their names,
some unknown souls
float around, sounds
echo off of walls
John and I wax politics,
art, word craft, madness.
Gravel Brothers tabled,
talk bikes, Tour Divide, wolves,
strong hearts climbing miles
and miles and miles.
My book party, Kansas weather.
Tiffany brings lager and smiles,
voices coalesce like a song
and I feel the scene,
melody of this place.
The pub pulses with people,
smiles bloom like wild
flowers, pedals unfolding
on Friday night
in the middle
of our town.

Life's Characters

Kerry Moyer

[midwest farm in winter]

Driving down pavement,
I pass a resting tractor
sunken into grass
near a friendly, old house
with a farmer
insulating
from the noise
of the world
with his faithful wife
in their simple home
blanketed, by the quiet
of a midwest winter

with Curtis Becker

Glenn's Knife

Glenn's knife, man's oldest
tool with ivory inlays, cut
from mammoth tusks buried
in earth, lost until river water
flowed, moved mud, exposed
what fell there before pyramids
were new. Tusks cut with steel
tools, machined, placed,
in a titanium slabbed handle.
A stainless, pointed blade, like
tusks, sharp, ancient art,
weapons, and my woolly-bearded
friend is buying a home,
on the east coast,
so Glenn sold me his knife
for a song.

Peyote

Years ago I ate
peyote. Apartment Shaman
across the hall brought
the things I shouldn't do.
We were in this small room,
and I'm in this brown recliner
that wouldn't let me go,
shrieking that this chair,
this sticky vinyl,
is eating me alive.
And I let go, let
go of every fear.

Red Chilean Wine

Red Chilean wine
passed between friends,
Mad Max snapped
pics and girls danced.
Cops showed up,
lights flashed red.
I leaned on their car,
asked to be cuffed,
offering them red
Chilean wine,
and they smiled,
Max clicking away,
cap still on the lens,
so, no pics and I
didn't go to jail.

Kerry Moyer

Breast Milk

She had long brown hair,
soft eyes behind glasses
and her child clung to her
breast, milk dripping
from a dark brown nipple
as she moved her child
to his blanket. I stared,
wide eyed. She smiled,
I looked away in wonder,
while she buttoned
her blouse.

[melody at night]

Jarrett's dancing hands
glide, touch keys while
Peacock plucks thick
bass strings, in time
with Jack's tapping
sticks as they glance
over his snare, these
tangential rivulets,
blue notes, downbeats,
this soft melody
at night.

Ink and Blood and Smoke

Ish and Led owned this
tattoo shop in Hutch, rode
Harley's, talked Sturgis,
and doing hard time.
Led inked this painted skull,
feathered tomahawk on my
right shoulder, says spirits
will lead me to glory, asks
if I'm holding. We burned
good weed in my marble
pipe while this shaman
colored my skin, like
some ancient ritual,
with ink and blood
and smoke.

[like horsepower]

Coffee shop talk,
caffeine like
horsepower, like
dual-exhaust
conversation, piston
heart pumps, pounds,
Mark comes in, we talk
clocks, muscle cars,
Kevin's Ford Mustang
Fastback, cops watching
him roll through town,
weaving, drag racing,
motors roar from memory
while my cold-brew
nitro flows, milk steams
and we are machines,
sitting strong, fueled,
until my phone rings,
wife tells me it's time
to say goodbye and leave.

Tangled

To drop like
a stone into
her, send waves
crashing heavy into
waiting banks, slow
ripples, caress
soft, supple shores,
where I get tangled,
held fast, lost
in forest waters,
her warm, flowing
waters.

Body

Kerry Moyer

[bionic]

Although I've ridden
over one hundred miles
over dirt, over gravel,
in a day, I wrecked my bike
popping a wheelie
on a quiet street,
my leg twisted
like a gnarled tree root
kept too long underwater.
My wife had to watch.
I can still hear
her scream. Now I wear
the knee brace, and tell
my nine year old
I'm bionic,
so he can't see
how I feel
weak, old, broken.

Bloody Knuckles

These cut, bloody
knuckles, trembling
hands, jackhammer
heart starts to slow
and I've won but
I'm numb, not sure
what this winning
means anymore.

Give Me Shoes

Give me shoes that can take
the weight, miles of this life.
Shoes with thick soles
leather from tough hide,
prairie- grazed cattle skin,
driven north from Texas,
Tanned, oiled to keep
feet warm, for storms to
pass over and still keep
feet dry for the walk, all
the miles ahead, for roads
I haven't seen yet or for paths
I have walked before.

[shower at 11:42 pm on a Tuesday]

Restless from the day
and my feet are tapping,
my mind a trap, snapping
sinapses like furious
lights flickering until
this idea finds me with
water thoughts, a hot
shower to wash me
clean of madness for
a time, until troubles
find me in need
of healing waters
again.

Kerry Moyer

Shower Chair

Warm drops explode against
my skull while water whirls
with a ugly sucking sound
down the drain and I breath
with no sense of time, my eyes
closed, and I'm numb, alone, while
water rolls over hunched shoulders.

I'm a mass of skin, hair, muscle,
bone, this gray shower chair holding
me up with a shriveled right leg, flat,
Deflated, against the rough plastic.
This medical chair, holds my spirit,
and I think this is what old and finished
must feel like.

[man in the...]

He is in the mirror
when I shave, the gray
hair dropping
to the sink, and when
I speak it is his voice
across years
and space. He rests
in the corners of my
eyes, his blue mingled
with mine. He is an echo.
I listen. I hear him.
I'll never be free.

Middle Age

I walk stiffer and my hands
ache after turning a wrench for a bit,
stacking logs to burn, by our fire pit.
I can't read labels well and need glasses.
I have comforts and space. I plan to live
here until I die. There is a quiet comfort,
a calm in that.

My yard is large and in one outbuilding
sits an old red tractor built in 1946,
the year my mother was born.
I tinker with it, think of time, how
this rusting steel machine
might outlive me, and Miles
might decide to keep it running.

I can still see muscle in my arms,
My legs can be spry when youth
calls me to kick a ball, or ride my bike.
My hands can make a fist and I've fought,
drawn blood. I can still feel dangerous
but age finds me gentle, slower
to let passions move me to anger.

I'm wise in ways, foolish in others,
I know to measure twice and cut
once. Hard miles have brought gray
to my hair, my beard. I walk my yard,
my stone fire pit is there, my large
stack of wood, ready
to be burned.

Mind

Kerry Moyer

[this box]

This box
I'm in
has thick
rock walls.
My hands,
they hammer,
make course
stone red
with blood
and I hear it,
this pounding
like a heartbeat,
like a savage,
relentless
drum.

Home

Home is a dream seen
through these eyes
and the ghosts that haunt
my walled in thoughts
whisper peace to this
warring heart, to a place
I've chased for so very long,
my feet are bruised,
my legs are tired
and I want to find a home
to lay my head, to lay
for a while,
wrapped in rest.

Concrete Shoes

Wearing concrete shoes
heavy feet plod through
grief and I keep walking
on these heavy feet
covered in concrete,
keeps me weighted
to these molded,
cement streets.

Wasteland

I want to rest my head
in soft thoughts, kind
illusions colored in the lying
pigment of wishful thinking.
I want to turn my eyes
from the dark spaces,
from this vast wasteland
creeping in from every side.

Surface Tension

The surface tension of water
is strong. Molecules cling,
bead together, form drops,
pool wherever they are close
to one another.
The man washed his face,
warm water on his hands,
while thoughts of her
flowed. Each one clung
to him. Warm, molecules
of her pooled around
his morning. Those
water thoughts, drops of her,
that surface tensions strong,
clinging to him while
he looked in the mirror
and water memories, like drops,
fell to the sink below.

Hamster Wheel

Hamster wheel turns
frantic revolutions
and I'm chasing this
thought that runs on the edge
of a blade, cut
and bleeding at the close
of this manic day.

Kerry Moyer

Waves

My small wooden boat
rolls on angry waves.
Heavy paddles dropped
from weary hands days ago,
sank into black waters.
I look up at the clever moon
and think she holds sway
over waves, the tides,
how she hides that ace
up her sleeve.

Rivulets

My day is water
rolling down glass,
thoughts like rivulets,
like cool, flowing streams,
running wherever
they choose
to go.

Tenpenny Nail

I'm a bent
ten-penny nail
sticking halfway
out of hardwood,
rusting, in this
thick, salty air.

Broken Notes

My life's a song played
on a broken guitar,
and in those notes
I find sweet, sweet
sounds, beautifully
broken notes in my
beautifully broken song.

[insomnia]

Hard thoughts hold
tired eyes open.
The world is
razors or roses
and either way
I bleed.

[ballerina]

I find the world to be hard,
relentlessly cruel, like
a ballerina being whipped
by razored tongues, screaming
notes, while spinning
on a bleeding, broken
toe.

Soul

Sacred

Give me something sacred,
a memory that feels holy,
a thought to build a life upon.

Give me a path to walk,
a path to wisdom,
a chance to talk with God.

[God, sometimes]

God,
sometimes
I am lonely, one
million miles, one
million thoughts from
anybody, and I know it's
bullshit and they are there,
but I don't want them, my
shell, like armor, like a wall
with thorns and covered
in ivy, blocking out light,
blocking out love, and it
is cold, so damn cold, like
frost on my shoulders, like
ice on my frozen heart.

Lost

Lord, sometimes I'm so
lost in the space between
words, like script, seeking
the next line of verse to
let my mind settle, to give
birth, the only way I can,
on a virgin page.

Dying

I think about dying
and some days it calls
me like a soft dream
floating by my
tired eyes.

Live and Let Live

"Live and let live"
I think that's nice,
fine, be like Christ,
kind, but then they
come at you—

with words.

with fists.

with hate.

If I Met the Devil

If I met the Devil
I'd challenge him to a duel,
ten paces and I'd cheat,
beat him at his own game.
I'd punch him in the face,
poke him in his evil eye,
for all the pain, for staining
our souls in the garden,
at the store, on the street,
in our homes, in church,
in our heads. I'd ask him
if he knows any of my
kin, If he pesters them,
if I'm damned for my sins.
I'd ask if I could take
a dip in the river Styx.
I would inquire if Virgil
was a guide for all
the new tenants,
if they scream hopeless
repentance, complain
about the rent. I'd ask him
why he didn't settle
for number two in heaven,
I'd tell him that vanity is folly.
I'd ask if he misses being loved
by God.
I'd ask if I could pray for him.

[in church]

The scent of mint
was Mother. Chewing
gum, like communion,
torn, broken, given
to my brother and me,
each of us, an equal share.
I'd smile, give thanks,
every Sunday.
And I knew, chewing
gum in church was
holy, like Mother's
love of God, as she
blessed each piece
held in the vessel
of her brown
leather purse.

Square Window

The sun, framed, setting in a squared
window, my thoughts turn to God and how
he spends his time. I wonder if he knows
I'm haunted and if he's watching
from the other side?

Kerry Moyer

Rings

Tree rings tell
of fires, floods,
easy years, hard
years with dark rings
deep and I'm a tree.
Can anyone read
my spirit rings?

Moyer Musings

Kerry Moyer

Like Morning

Espresso machine
spits. Barista whips
foam. She pours
hot milk. There is
a chatter. Coffee
cups clatter, clang,
a hum. This place
smells like morning.

Coffee

Coffee starts my day.
Coffee, liquid ecstasy.
How you enslave me.

Sharp Edges

The house had sharp edges,
sharp corners, housed sharp,
jagged, parents, sharp-edged
hands, looks, sharp words cut
the children, their soft skin cut
and bled, souls bled, their cries
bleeding, cut and bleeding,
everywhere sharp eyes see
people with sharp, cutting
edges, corners, sharp
sounds, voices cutting
out the heart of youth,
the heart of hope.

Chewing Sounds

Chewing sounds
bounce off of brown
shabby walls, metal
forks on white plates,
scraping for stray olives,
ice cubes fall into cups.
Lines pile their plates,
like Roman's at a feast,
hunched over, chewing,
pizza sauce on chins,
piles of crumpled red
spattered napkins,
flushed faces, heavy
breathing, heavy forks,
heavy lumbering
for three more slices
and I see some starving
kid from an infomercial
swarmed with flies in my
mind and I'm hunched over
my plate, breathing heavy
with a stack of empty plates
like a tower of shame
inches from my chewing face.

Letter Jacket

I gave my letter jacket—
blue with white leather
sleeves—to an ex-con,
along with three shirts
and a pair of shoes,
and he was clean, and
he was grateful, and I saw
him strung out, three years
later, high out of his mind,
and there he was, shaking
in a chill November breeze,
and I think, I bet you wish
that jacket was still around,
and he looked right at me,
through me, like I wasn't
even there.

Fireflies

When the fireflies light up
and flicker outside
my window, I am drawn.
The radio plays notes
from folk songs bowed
across fiddles.
Barefoot girls spin
while boys stomp
dust floors, guitars pickin',
droppin' notes in mason jars.
I see ghosts singin' hymns,
songs about white
lightning and longing,
dreams, mountain
streams, places they
will never see again.
And those fireflies
flicker, glow, dim
like prayers
outside my window
below a waning moon.

Flim-Flam

Nostalgia is a technicolor lie,
a commercial and I buy it.
We have this phony used-car
salesman's flim-flam world.
Everywhere I look, it's all
for sale. Everyone has a price
and we stand slack- jawed,
waiting to be bought, waiting
to be told our worth, only
to get sold in the bargain bin.

Wooden Box

I have a wooden box
of knives and guns
and I watch the news,
hear that preacher say
bad men are coming,
but I got a wooden box
of knives and guns
and goddamn if I
don't hear 'em coming.

Trench Warfare

Mud, blood,
barbed wire,
out in no-man's land
and I'm crouched, hidden
behind sand bags
in this trench, at war
with my nature,
waiting for the whistle
that will send me over
the top, to be covered
in mud, blood, tangled
in barbed wire that cuts,
holds me there,
always right there.

A Kansas Life

Kerry Moyer

[sitting in my truck at a railroad crossing]

I sit in my truck at a railroad
crossing. Red lights flash at dusk
while two engines pull tattooed boxcars
that stretch, disappearing around
a bend. This steel snake traveling
over miles of steel tracks,
bringing goods to us.

Hot rolled rails cross patch-work fields,
cattle pastures, they twist through concrete,
steel cities, plywood towns where people hear
whistles wailing off in in the distance.
Trains move like blood,
coursing through
my country.

Leaves

Leaves blow into my garage,
the slightest sound comes
with them, they are friends
today, reminding me of change
and giving a task, for later,
to pass quiet time
with my broom.

Colors tumble while
this broom moves
fall's remains back
to this Kansas breeze,
so they may come back
to me when a south wind
delivers them again.

Kerry Moyer

Sidewalk Quiet

I found sidewalk quiet,
my red sneakers soft
on gray concrete and my
thoughts are wrapped up
in counting cracks with each
step, while I wander block
after block and I'm walking
for nothing but quiet,
to find sidewalk quiet,
away from people
and what troubles
my heart today.

Trees in the Fall

I walk my yard,
watch trees undress,
dropping yellow leaves,
that float to the ground
and I think, the chill brings
rest, their burden of growth
and green gives way to sleep
for now, until this coming spring
where I think, we may grow
together with water, warmth
light, our roots holding
fast to the earth.

[Do you shop here often?]

I'm busting out
of my skin, an
unfettered scream erupts
from the middle of
me. A sound from
my soul's bones.
It is the noise, being
trapped.

I'm a cornered cat.

Coming back to my
senses, I tell the young,
blonde gum-chewing
clerk that I'm paying
with cash, followed
by a smile and nod
to the uncomfortable
woman behind me in line
who gives me side-eye,
with that, I turn and ask,

"Do you shop here often?"

God & Lattes

My nitro
cold brew is
both bitter
and sweet,
like a muted
Miles Davis solo, like
Kansas weather, when
you don't know
if it will rain. I sip
coffee with James,
who knows jazz
better than women,
and I think, if God
were here, he'd
also have a latte
and talk only of jazz
and wait
for big clouds
to roll in.

with Kevin Rabas

Fortune Cookie

Cold Chinese take out
in white waxy bags
and duck sauce on
a Wednesday. Fortune
cookie is cracked
and the little white
paper rectangle says
something about
being generous.
I think about the guy
that brought me food,
and how I'd tipped
him two dollars.
Chewing the hard
semi-sweet treat, I think,
what the hell does a random
damn cookie know
about my life anyway?

Red Barn

A red barn leans,
the red paint flakes from its hide,
time chips it away, battered
with wind and rain.

A wild green claims its victims:
a white farmhouse,
three mangled sheds
left empty with broken
windows, sagging roofs.

I feel drawn to this place,
and always slow my pace,
look and listen for whispers
from a past I will never see.
A past that always calls to me.

Garden Song

She worked soil,
dirty hands pulled
weeds away from
wanted reds, greens
and sweat shown
slick on shoulders,
arms, legs, darkened
under a fierce yellow
sun, and the young
man saw her lips
singing a melody he
learned that summer,
her garden song planting
passion's seed in his
wild, fevered dreams.

One Day

One day, I will die,
my body burned,
turned to embers,
like tallgrass prairie,
set ablaze in that
coming spring,

Floating ash will cling to
buzzing bees, busy bringing
pollen to waiting blooms,
for sweet nectar, that will
become honey to eat.

My dust will whirl, dance
with soot, seed, smoke,
settle in dirt, wait for rains,
where new life will grow,
in the rich prairie earth
of Kansas.

Kerry Moyer

Prairie Heart

Two towers reach toward
blue skies from their prairie
home, rooted in limestone,
in earth, and the north wind
is soft like a cotton cloud,
a whisper while I pedal
my bike up rock, around
puddles from recent rains
and the noise of town
is behind me, far from
my thoughts, far from
this prairie heart.

About the Author

Kerry Moyer resides in Emporia Kansas with his wife Sarah and their boys Edward and Miles. Kerry is the author of two Chapbooks "Let's Start with That" and "these boys" along with poetry collections Dirt Road and Rust & Weeds. He is an active member of Kansas Author's Club and the Emporia Writer's Group and is on KAC's State Board serving as Prose Contest Manager. A trained suicide prevention and intervention instructor, Kerry became involved with Beacon for Hope a non-profit suicide prevention organization and currently serves on the board. He also serves on the Board of the William Allen White Foundtion and directs Arterial Ink, a fundraising literary journal supporting the foundation. Kerry has worked in community mental health working with youth and young adults for twenty years and is currently a Crisis Prevention and Intervention Instructor, Mental Health First Aid Instructor and Pediatric CPR/First Aid instructor. Other intrests include cycling where he has participated in gravel cycling events like the Dirty Kanza/Unbound Gravel race which calls Emporia and the Flint Hills home. Kerry also holds a fifth-degree black belt in Taekwondo and first-degree black belt in Hapkido. "Master Moyer" taught martial arts and self-defense for over a decade and continues to be sporadically involved in the martial arts world. Kerry enjoys creating arts and crafts as well as playing music on his guitar when he can. Kerry is inspired as a writer by the people, communities, and landscapes of Kansas and the Midwest.

A Note of Thanks

I'd like to thank my family and friends who have supported my writing over the years, especially this last year and a half. I can say that their support has been all the difference during this difficult period of our history. I want to thank my friend and publisher, **Curtis Becker** of **Kellogg Press** for continuing to support my poetry and be there for me as a human being. He has made this an easier road than it might have been otherwise. To **Kevin Rabas**, I've gotta say, "Thank you brother, for your friendship and being my Yoda." I am a better poet due in no small part to your influence. Thank you to **Kansas Authors Club** and **Emporia Writers Group** for the friendships and support over the years. I'd like to thank the **Flint Hills**, **Emporia**, and my beloved **Kansas** for continuing to inspire me to share my thoughts through the medium of poetry. To my wife **Sarah** and our boys **Edward** and **Miles**, you are my heart. I know that I'm not always easy to navigate but know my north star always guides me home to you.

Much Love-KM

Also Available from Kellogg Press

Vacant Childhood
Lindsey Bartlett

He Watched and Took Note
Curtis Becker

Six Feet Apart: Poetry from the Pandemic
AJ Dome

Everything is Ephemera
Dennis Etzel, Jr.

Dirt Road
Kerry Moyer

Rust & Weeds
Kerry Moyer

I Love the Child
Ronda Miller

Winds of Time
Ronda Miller

Watch Your Head
Kevin Rabas

Watch Your Head 2
Kevin Rabas

Lessons from the Trials of Life
Carl Rice

Order online at kelloggpress.com